Love Always

Glory's Way

Gloria Jean Powers

AmErica House
Baltimore

© 2001 by Gloria Jean Powers.

All rights reserved. No part of this book may be reproduced in any form without written permission from the publishers, except by a reviewer who may quote brief passages in a review to be printed in a newspaper or magazine.

First printing

Photo done by: Tom Baird

ISBN: 1-58851-697-0
PUBLISHED BY AMERICA HOUSE
BOOK PUBLISHERS
www.publishamerica.com
Baltimore
Printed in the United States of America

Dedications

I first thank God and the Power in the Universe.

Special Friends:
Don, Lee, and Hayley DuMond,
for their "Spiritual Connection"
in helping make this book possible.

Also:
For the love and support of
Vic and Judy Baus

Special Recognition to:
Ho-Hum RV Park,
which was the old Gulf Breeze RV Park
where most of this book takes place.
What a wonderful few years it was living there.

My husband:
Danny L. Husk, Sr.
For his years of love, support, and understanding,
and also our children:
Danny, Jr., Richard, Johnny, and Kathrina.

My father and mother:
Benton Glenn Powers, Sr. and Oneita Mae Karickhoff

My brothers and sisters:
Pamela Mae (Powers) Moore, Debra Kay (Powers) Quick,
Benton Glenn, Jr., Thomas Wayne Powers,
and Connie Susan (Powers) Nelson

I love you all.

Contents

CHAPTER I: Gloria By The Sea — 7

CHAPTER II: A Walk With Thee — 43

CHAPTER III: Special Memories — 75

CHAPTER IV: Love Is Free — 107

CHAPTER V: Together Once Again — 139

CHAPTER I

GLORIA BY THE SEA

The Bay	9
Sunset	10
Sunrise	12
A Dolphin's Tail	13
Dream Voyage	14
Shrimp Boat	16
A Fishless Tale	17
Pinkie	18
Lost At Sea	21
The Fisherman	24
Disaster Afloat	25
Pellie	26
Island Dreams	27
Soar Of Eagles	28
Nature's Call	30
Rainbow Bay	32
A New Morning	34
Moonlit Night	35
Wake Rider	36
Host Of A Ghost	37
Death of the Bay	39
The River	40

The Bay

There is no place so beautiful, as the bay
Which is consuming, every day

Of which there are, some islands three
That are stretched out, so long and free

One of which is St. George
Which has a bridge you can forge

Another one is Dog
Which at times gets lost in fog

The littlest one, is Bird
Of which it is, third

Also there is a reef
Which can, give some grief

Its name is Lanark
Where boats accidentally park

1-21-1995

Sunset

As it rises, it will set
With so much beauty, you can bet

The colors burst across, the sky
With so much, glory, you ask not why

The sky, is so aglow,
With its, own light show

The water, comes alive, with such hues
Of, so many blues

A pink,
That, will really, make you think

The red,
It goes, right, to your head

Yellow,
It's for, a dreamy fellow

Your, eyes are lit,
With, such, violet

Even as the, sun goes down
You, can not, frown

Because, to come, soon,
There, will be, the moon

Like it, there is, no other
The time, to spend, with your lover

1-21-1995

Sunrise

The sun rises, every day
Always in, a different way

It is so bright, and bold
It shines as bright, as yellow gold

The rays from above, will flow
As it makes, the water glow

The water, looks, as though, it will dance
To look away, I will not chance

For as it rises, in the sky
It is so beautiful, to the eye

Now as it goes, up so high
It's time to, say good-bye

1-21-1995

A Dolphin's Tail

Oh! What a "beautiful sight"
As the, dolphin's tail, flips! like a bird, in flight

They twirl and whirl, at a glance
Like a ballerina's dance

The attentive mother and child
Play and flip! so wild

They circle on, schools of fish
That makes a tasty dish

Waiting, to be fed
Gulls, circle, overhead

And when they are done
I can say, it sure has been fun

They'll come again, another day
For me, to watch, them play

3-15-1995

Dream Voyage

To find, a dream come true
Is what, I have with you

The day, we met
I never, will forget

You fall, into my heart
Now, we'll never part

Our love, runs deep and wide
And over flows, like a tide

You carried, me away
On, that beautiful day

Upon a schooner white
It was, a sailor's, delight

With, great sails and masts
Rigged, both, fore and aft

On the Glory B., just you and me
Sailing, across the sea

Oh! How nice
To be, in paradise

Beauty, beyond belief
Anchored, above the reef

And as we sail, the dolphins, look so brave
As they ride, upon the wave

From, the crow's nest
I see, an island rest

I loved, the cove
Where, we dove

As, we cavort
We dream, of our, next port

The biggest wave, can't wash away
Our love, that's here, to stay

4-18-1995

Shrimp Boat

By day, they make not a peep
For that, is when they sleep

Big and white and well made
They all go on parade

By night, they light the bay
Like a great causeway

As they go along, dragging net and door
Back and forth, across the ocean floor

Like great crabs
They come up, with big grabs

Being a shrimper, is a hard life
Especially, being away, from his wife

While fishing, I saw, ones name on the back
It was called, "Variety Pack"

4-21-1995

A Fishless Tale

Floating, along in the bay
While, fishing one day

I took, a quick look
I had one! on the hook

There he was, on the line,
Which, was so fine

He, took off, so bold,
He, made it, hard to hold

He pulled, the line, so tight
Putting up, such a fight

With my lure, in his mouth
He, headed south

But then, it doubled back
Breaking, the line with a whack

All, that was seen
Was, a bright silver sheen

Needless, to say,
The fish, got away

5-1-1995

Pinkie

One day, a storm blew in
Her name, was Allison

The winds, blew hard
Everyone, was on guard

It blew up, a gale
As its winds, did wail

Then, it was gone,
Just after dawn

Left, in its wake,
A life, it didn't take

A beautiful! pink flamingo
With, nowhere to go

I wonder about, its fate
Because, it has no mate

In, its new home,
Now, it does roam

Its, beauty and grace
Puts a smile, on my face

6-14-1995

***

A TROPICAL VISITOR
BLOWS INTO THE BIG BEND

A FLAMINGO HANGING OUT NEAR LANARK VILLAGE FLORIDA MAY HAVE HITCHED A RIDE ON HURRICANE ALLISON

For the first time in 23 years, a pink flamingo has turned up in North Florida, a probable rider on the storm called Allison.

The 4-foot tall bird, native to Caribbean Islands and Central and South America, hasn't been reported in this part of the state since one spent the day at St. Marks lighthouse on June 19, 1972.

Wildlife biologist Jeff Gore said the bird has been feeding along the shoreline at Lanark Village the past week or so, and the Game and Freshwater Fish Commission is trying to determine whether it's wild or an escapee from a private collection. As of Wednesday, no one had reported it missing, and the flamingo shows signs of being wild, he said. "It doesn't have a leg band. And its feathers are not worn, and it's shy," Gore said. "That leads us to think it may have been nudged up here by hurricane Allison from one of the Caribbean Islands or Yucatan Peninsula."

According to the book "The Bird Life of Florida" by the late Henry Stevenson and Bruce Anderson, flamingos never were native to Florida, except possibly the keys. There is no convincing evidence wild flamingos have bred in Florida since 1901.

The book indicates that wild flamingos at Everglades

National Park probably migrated from Cuba, the Bahamas or a captive population in Hialeah. They sometimes wander along the Gulf of Mexico and Atlantic coasts.

Eddie White, an avid bird watcher who works for the Game and Fish Commission's Division of Wildlife, said, "Flamingos are peculiar birds."

"A flamingo's tongue is attached to the roof of its mouth instead of the bottom like other animals," he said. "That enables flamingos search for food with their heads upside down. They probe around under water for small fish, aquatic invertebrates and algae, which they filter out by forcing water out of their bills. A flamingo's diet causes its pink coloration. Without adequate marine life in their food supply, flamingos tend to turn white in captivity," White said.

Although flamingos aren't classified as native to Florida, state and federal laws protect them as migratory birds. Anyone who harms a wild flamingo could face a $500 fine and six months in jail.

Taken from:
TALLAHASSEE DEMOCRAT
Thursday, June 22, 1995
BY: Henry Cabbage
DEMOCRAT WRITER

Lost At Sea

On this, beautiful day
They did, motor away

A plan, they did hatch
To come home, with a catch

But along, the way
That, beautiful day

The motor, gave out
Someone did shout!

The tide, carried them away
On that, fateful day

Where their days and nights
Were full, of fright!

As the land
Was near, at hand

They shot a flare
Into the air

A, fishing boat
Was soon, afloat

With, little green boat, in tow
They had, not far to go

Safe, back on land
They, kissed the sand

Now, they are all, safe from harms
Back, in their, family's arms

They thanked, the fishing, boat's crew
That, nobody knew

The Lord, above
That, gave them, hope and love

6-15-1995

* * *

LOST AT SEA

APALACHICOLA COUPLES TOWED TO SAFETY YANKEETOWN, FLORIDA.

Two Apalachicola couples adrift nearly three days in a disabled 18-foot boat were in good health Wednesday after a fishing boat towed them in to Horseshoe Beach, the Coast Guard said.

The small green boat with a beige bimini top floated 90 nautical miles from Panama City in the central panhandle nearly to the shore of Dixie County on the northern peninsula, Coast Guard spokesman Dan McDonald said.

Officials who interviewed the four at a Horseshoe Beach fish house after their rescue found them, "a little hungry and thirsty but otherwise ok," said officer Richard Hutchinson.

A flare from the boat was sighted at 4:45 a.m. Wednesday, seven miles southwest of Horseshoe Beach by the fishing boat Specalec, which towed the disabled craft into port.

At least three Coast Guard planes as well as Coast Guard and Florida Marine Patrol boats had scoured the Gulf of Mexico since Gary and Jeanette McIntosh, Laurie Cameron and Tim Collins were reported missing Monday by family members. The four told officials they had drifted since their boat's 115 horsepower outboard engine developed trouble about 5 p.m. Sunday.

Taken from:
The Oyster Radio Newsroom
6-15-1995

The Fisherman

He wakes, before dawn
And before you know it, he's gone

With favorite, fishing pole
He's off, to his favorite hole

Looking for bass
In all, the tall grass

To lose, a big red
He would, really dread

He has, no doubt
He will, catch a trout

With his, catch of the day
That he, caught in the bay

His dinner tonight
Will be, a delight

7-2-1995

Disaster Afloat

The bay
Was, calm that day

The most beautiful, sail boat
Was afloat

Her sails, billowed, in the wind
As a sailor, up the mast, he did ascend

But on that morning
Without warning

The boat was tossed, to and fro
As the waves, they did grow

The boat, they did smash!
With a terrible, crash!

Over! she went
To her, great descent

Now, on the bottom, she lay
Since, that fateful day

7-20-1995

Pellie

Pellie was, my friendly, little pelican
But not a friend, to all man

I remember, the day we met
I was out, throwing my net

I would go out, to catch bait
And before long, Pellie had it ate

There was many a time; he came to the door
He would look up, as if to ask for more

He would stay, by the trailer, to guard
Like a dog, in his own yard

Everyone thought, he was a trip
But on him, no one, could get a grip

But! then came the day
Then there was, no more play

Pellie had sealed his fate
He had, found a mate

8-5-1995

Island Dreams

There is a road, along the sea
I wished the road, brings you back to me

To bury our toes, in the sand
As we walk, the beach, hand in hand

The winds, whisper and rejoice
At the sound, of your gentle voice

And there is, the voice, of the island's call
That haunts, me most of all

To lie upon, the white sand beach
With coconuts, at our reach

On the island's, fruit, we dine
And I feel your love, as we entwine

And to watch, the gentle sway, of the palm
As we're filled, with peace and calm

But then I wake, with the dawn
To find it's a dream, and that you're gone

Was it a dream? Or was I really there?

8-15-1995

Soar of Eagles

To watch an, eagle soar
Will only, make you, ask for more

They fly up high, the air to ride
And catch a pocket, there to glide

They fly across, the bay so wide
Still looking, for that, air to ride

Along the way, a fish they spot
From way up there, it's just a dot

Around and round they soar
They look and look and soar some more

And all of a sudden, they start to hover
And the poor fish, runs for cover

Then he takes his shot, he makes a dash
The eagle dives, with such a splash

When he, emerges, from the sea
He flies away, so wild and free

With fish in hand,
He flies to land

To find their nest,
Where babies rest

Now, as the sun, goes away
They wait, for another day

8-20-1995

Nature's Call

I see the beauty, of a clear blue sky
In the mountains, up so high

I feel the breeze, upon my face
As I explore, this peaceful place

I hear the chatter, of a squirrel
As he gives, his tail a whirl

I listen to, the untold words
Of the beautiful, song birds

I hear the rustle, of a tree
That stands, so tall and free

I see the ripple, of a brook
As I climb down, to take a look

I follow the brook, to a stream
Where the water, it does gleam

Last but not least
I catch a fish, for my dinner feast

As the sun, goes out of sight
I bed down, for the night

I lay there, to fall asleep
My mind, in thought so deep

My thoughts say! "We're so far apart"
"I love you""Good night sweet heart"

8-5-1995

Rainbow Bay

"Crystal blue"
All I do, is think of you
When I see, the crystal blue
Of, my ocean view

"Emerald green"
A most, beautiful scene
Is when, the sea, turns emerald green
It's the brightest, ever seen

"Purple haze"
Much to my amaze
There comes, a purple haze
Upon which, I do gaze

"Yellow gold"
There is, a sea so bold
It shines, of yellow gold
To gaze upon it, never grows old

"Hot pink" while you sit and think
You dare, not blink
For you might miss, a pink, I think

What more can I say!
When the colors of the bay

Come into view, at the end of the day
Except! I wish I could send, them all your way

11-5-1995

A New Morning

There is, no better, place to be
Than living, by the sea

To open, my eyes
To a new, sunrise

As I awaken
There's the scent, of bacon

Fresh oranges, to squeeze
In the morning breeze

To have my coffee
And feel so free

To start, a brand new day
And hope to view it, in a special way

12-4-1995

Moonlit Night

One moonlit night
My feet, took flight

I walked along, the white sand beach
My thoughts of you, within my reach

The sand, like diamonds, at my feet
I thought I'd walk, until we meet

Looking out, across the bay
If only, I could see you, come my way

Just then! I swell with tear
Knowing! you're nowhere near

My memories of you, I held that night
As I "walked alone", in the "bright moon light"

1-4-1996

Wake Rider

While going out to sea
I looked in front of me

I saw a swirl
And gave my head a whirl

Looking along side the boat
I saw its gray coat

A dolphin! I saw that day
He swam ahead and darted back, to play

I looked down and had to do, a double take
Cause! there he was, riding the wake

Looking as though he had a smile
He swam along for a while

And all of a sudden! with a dart
He did depart

1-10-1996

Host of A Ghost

The sea,
Is no place to be

With the fog,
It looks like a spooky bog

Off in the distance
Someone may, need assistance

Cause! I heard, the eerie sound
Of a boat, that ran aground

But! just then I heard, the motor roar
And the boat, headed for shore

I wished the fog, would set it free
Cause there was nothing, I could see

With a blast,
The boat moved fast

All of a sudden!! it broke the fog
Headed straight! For a log

It's not going to stop!! it would seem
So I started to scream!!!

With a quick will
The motor, they did kill

And they fell back
As the boat, gave a whack!!!

They gave an OK shout!!!
They turned about, and headed back out

Like a dream, it would all seem

And the fog, was host,
To an eerie ghost

2-22-1996

Death of the Bay

There came a day
Across the bay

When came a cloud
An eerie shroud

The smell of death
Did take, my breath

Everyone would dread
This cloud of red

It worked up the coast
Like an eerie ghost

And it would take
Everything in its wake

Nowhere to run! Nowhere to hide!
They were caught, in its red tide!

So many fish, of a different kind
No safe place, could they find

Gasping their last breath!
They go! to their fateful death

6-12-1996

The River

The river comes, the river goes
It always winds, it always flows

The water deep, the water dark
Oh! How it will, hark

Along its bank, an egret
Its beauty, you can't forget

Along the way, a gator
That you may, see later

A little turtle
Playing in mud, so fertile

How peaceful
The flight, of a gull

The quiet perched, pelican
Has the look, a little old, man can

The grass blowing, in the wind
Like the welcome, wave of a friend

Somewhere, just around the bend
The river holds, another friend

But in the distance, I see the sea
Where it winds, to be set free

2-24-1995

CHAPTER II

A WALK WITH THEE

Mother Dear	45
Star Bright Feather	48
A Brother's Love	51
Heaven Bound	52
A Message of Love	53
My Angel	55
God's Gentle Touch	56
Jenny Flying Free	59
The Gate Keeper	61
Swept Away	63
Reflections	65
Spirits Dancing	67
God's Office Door	68
Full Circle	70
My Child of God	72
The Valley Green	74

Mother Dear

There was a day, while by the bay,
Talking to a lady, from far away

She told, of a day, that was so bad,
That, it made her sad

The love, of a mother,
Is like that, of no other.

She had a son,
With whom, she had fun

But, then one day,
Everything, became gray

When the son, with whom, she had fun,
Was killed with a gun

The mother, dressed in, black lace, with pain, on her face
"Says" to her son, go to God, with grace

The son named Mark,
Now, with the angels, does hark

It, has been a while,
There, has been no smile

But, I know, in my heart,
They, will never part

And that Mark, is happy, as a lark
And now, she can, come out of the dark

As he, surrounds her, with love,
From, up above

The days, will be bright, as he, helps her, to see the light
And she will always, love him, with all, her might

Mother dear! Have, no fear,
I will, always be near

3-27-1995

* * *

"Mother Dear"

A Tribute to Mark

This is another very unusual thing that happened one day.
Thank you Lisa and Jerry
Thank you Mark for the touch from above

   I had met this lady one day who seemed to have so much pain and sorrow about her.
   Later we had some polite conversation. Later that night I still was having an odd feeling. A little later I started the poem. When I gave the poem to Lisa the next day, she read it and

started to cry. Then she told me how true it was, what I had written. We just sat there holding each other, crying. Then she told of seeing Mark before he was cremated. She said he looked nice and tan, with a warm beautiful smile on his face. She said it felt as though there was a warm glow surrounding them and that she felt he was at peace, but when it was all over, the human factor started.

It has been very hard on her; Mark was an only child. It was weird, cause while I was going through the feelings, I was writing the poem and next door Lisa and Jerry were going through a weird thing, too. Jerry was reading, and Lisa asked him, at three different times, "Did you call to me?" She had heard someone call "Mother." Jerry hadn't said a word. While back next door with me, I was being torn between the words "mom" and "mother." Well, it turned out I put down "mother." In my opinion there were some forces at work that night, (believe it or not). Lisa had also told me that she considered this to be a sign of love and hope from Mark and for her to have no fear, that he was fine. This was the first time she had had a sign from him since he died.

Lisa also told me that Jerry couldn't stand to see Mark before he was cremated. He just wanted to keep the lasting memory of Mark being alive and well; you can't blame him for that. I do feel Mark is at peace in his universe.

Star Bright Feather

I saw a feather, float today,
As I sailed, across the bay

So soft and white,
And shone so bright

But later this eve,
Was a time to grieve

It was a time to mourn,
A bright star, that had been born

Born of peace and love,
From up above

Held in the hands, that hold her dear,
Now lets her go, without fear

Loves bright star,
Now shines from afar

Her time,"now" on Earth is done,
Now with God, will be one

And "now" there is a special place,
For this "nameless", little face

Now she travels, through the night,
In the "warmth of God's Holy Light"

So until then,"Mom and Dad",
Look to the stars and don't be sad

The day will come, we "reunite",
Again, "in God's Holy Light"

And when you see, a "feather fall"
Remember! she had, "God's Special Call"

But to me, "she" will be known
As the, "brightest star", ever shown
And the, "lightest feather", ever flown

1-5-1996

* * *

From Grandmother Of Little Star Bright Feather
To my son Danny and daughter-in-law Angel and grandson Garrett

STAR BRIGHT FEATHER

A little angel that God needed more than we did. We love you, baby girl.

We had a phone call from our son Danny Jr. He told of how his wife had lost their second baby.

It was born premature; it died while he held it in his hands. It was so premature that the hospital advised that they themselves take of it. So they gave our son a certificate of birth and bracelet but no name. It was so hard to deal with that, happening the way it did. We had been out on the boat that day; I had seen a beautiful white feather floating on the water and that evening the stars were shining bright. Then the call came.

A Brother's Love

Against all strife
We went through life

And on something, I could count
Of that, I had no doubt

Of my brother's love
Sent from above

As children, we would pick and tease
But in the end, always meant to please

Our mom and dad, with love in their face
Always! taught us, of God's Love and Grace

Now! you're no longer, near
My brother dear and have no fear

God! holds you close, in His arms
And shields, you from all harms

So till, that glorious day
That, God! brings me your way

Watch over me, from up above
Wrapped in the arms, of God's Holy Love

10-3-1996

Heaven Bound

He came, upon this land
With God's, Loving Hand

Now! This person, of great wealth
Is of ailing health

He didn't have anyone, to really care
Or even know he was there

This man! so all alone!
Didn't have anyone, to call his own

That day, he passed away
Now! in the church he lay

There a prayer was said
By a man God had led

This man of love and grace
Knew not! What he would face

The wealthy man
Had made a plan

That his wealth would be spent
On the friend, that God had sent

10-3-1996

A Message of Love

A son got a message, from up above
To tell his mother, of his love

Not knowing, what was in store
He wouldn't see, her anymore

For on that day,
There would come his way

On its "evil course",
A deadly force

To take this son,
From everyone

Everyone! but! God that is!
For he had claimed, the boy as his

And now he waits, up there on high
For his parents by and by

P.S. "I love you"

The loving hand, of God is near
To teach you all, to never fear

The love of God, will! see you through
For His "love is always true"

Today I went through heaven's gate
And there for you! "I will wait"

In memory of the loving spirit of Charles Russell Yates
That I feel I met through his parents
Carmen & Ferrell Yates
At Gulf Breeze RV Park, Carrabelle, Florida

10-9-1996

* * *

The Meeting of Charles Yates' Parents

    The day that they came to the park, the most visible thing of them was a wheel cover on their Bronco with the words, "Our son was murdered at Burger King" and their phone number. Not much was said, but a polite "Hi!" from afar. The next day I was throwing my net for bait, and they walked down to the water to see what I was doing. As they got closer, they asked what I was doing, so I told and showed them.

    The man went back to the car; the woman came closer to talk to me. As she got closer to me, I felt what I call a "Warm Fuzzy Feeling" as she stopped in front of me. There it went again: that head-to-toe feeling. It was all I could do to keep it together and talk to her. As soon as I got done putting up my things, I went in and wrote "a message of love." It took about fifteen minutes and it was done. Before they left I gave them a copy of it, and they gave me copies from the newspaper and a letter they had written. They said the murder trial was coming up in November. They said they were trying to rest up to be able to face it.

    God and Charles be with you.
10-9-1996

My Angel

My angel! if we're far apart
I'll always! hold you in my heart

I do believe, as I grow older
I have an angel, on my shoulder

With my eyes, open wide
I have my angel, for a guide

I feel! when I grow, old and gray
He'll be there, to light the way

For some reason, I feel I must
"Place in him all my trust"

10-20-1996

God's Gentle Touch

A day at the beach
Was just out of reach

As they drove
Down and around the cove

Along the bay
On that beautiful day

A man and his daughter out for fun
In the beauty of the noonday sun

But! unknown to them, that day
There was danger, on its way

Two teens, had stolen a car
They were down the way, not too far

In hot pursuit! were the cops
Their speeds were tops

As they rounded the turn, they lost control
Hit the girl and her dad and started to flip and roll

I heard the crash
And took off like a flash

As I got there, the girl and a friend,
Were sitting on the edge of the road
My heart suddenly sank with a heavy load

As I saw her dad lying on the ground
With people starting to gather round

All looking at them, with dismay
As on the ground he did lay

I did not stop or hesitate
But went to his side, to wait his fate

And from us there came no, sign of fear
Because Lord the Father, He was near

I gave comfort by his side
Till in the ambulance, he did ride

His daughter and her friend two
Were still quite blue

When they had spoken to her grandmother, by phone
Their voices began, to change tone

I gave them a kiss, on the cheek
They then left with a policeman, with which they did speak

As I went home, I started to cry
As I prayed, they'd be OK! by and by

4-3-1997

* * *

God's Gentle Touch

One day while sitting in the RV, we heard a big crash out on the highway. I took off running out the door. I didn't even stop to think how bad it may have been. I ran past everyone else that was there.

Two cars were there; one was upside down. There I saw a man laying half out of the upside down car. I went right to him, and he asked about his daughter and her friend. They had kicked out the window and went to sit at the edge of the road with Toni, one of the owners of the RV Park. I set there holding the man. I know he was hurting bad; so was I with my back and joints. I remember saying to myself, "Oh! God, please help me with him," and thinking back on it at the time, I felt no more pain. I heard him gurgling a few times; I remember asking God to let him be OK because I was afraid of internal injury. A half-hour later they put him on a stretcher and took him away. When I got back to the RV, I was like a wet noodle, tired and shaky. We had no idea what had happened with him but asked God to look out for him.

He really did because he and his mom came looking for me the next day; it was her car he wrecked. And it wasn't even his fault; some boys had stolen a car and were running from the police, passed on the turn and crashed him head-on. Thank God everything turned out OK!

4-3-1997

Jenny Flying Free

Like an injured bird
Jenny lay waiting for the word

The word from thee,
That would set her free

"Free"
Free for to be with thee

Free like a butterfly on the wind,
With a message to send

A message to the heart,
That we will never be apart

The message came one day,
While there she lay

The angels from up above,
Came swooping like a dove

To gently carry her away,
On that wonderful day

A day that many they would mourn
But for Jenny she was not forlorn

For in an instant she was set free to fly
To meet us again in the by and by

Now her beautiful spirit will glow
As on the winds it will flow

Or see her in the beauty of a pure white butterfly
As like a beautiful angel she flutters by

Whole and free,
She flies with thee

Now you hold her close to thee
Thank You Jesus for setting Jenny free

8-24-1997

    After reading a letter from Hackers Creek Pioneer Descendants, Inc., my hometown genealogy source, about a lady, Jenny (Shaffer) Jones, who was dying of cancer, I wrote this.

The Gate Keeper

He would stand and watch and wait
This keeper of the gate

Watching and waiting for someone's next of kin
To hold out a hand and welcome them in

He worked in an RV park
Where he watched, from daylight to dark

As they came in, to find their space
He always, had a smile on his face

He went about, his daily deed
Caring, for your every need

But now, the gate is empty there
Of which, he took, so much care

For you see, he passed on, the other night
He gave up, and went to God's Holy Light

For God's call, he did wait
So he could guard, the pearly gate

And meet his kin
They're within

It's sad for us, this is true
But now, with God, he's made anew

IN MEMORY OF: ROBERT (BOB) EMERSON
Who was the manager of the Ho Hum RV Park,
where we lived at the time; we're now across the street.

9-19-1997

Swept Away

I was told a story the other day,
And much to my dismay

It happened, on a Sunday morn,
Emotions, they were quite torn

Some people came, from far away,
To hold a service, by the bay

They brought with them an urn full of ash
With a prayer and a breeze, the ashes, were gone in a flash

And after all, was said and done,
They all drove off, into the sun

But as the story was told, by Mike
To the end of the pier, he took a hike

As he reached the end he thought! "What the heck!"
There! "laying on the deck"

Were! "the ashes of Don Hess",
Oh! boy! what a mess!

Was this poor guy, still hanging around
And know he wasn't put in the ground

There was no time to waste,
He was swept away with haste

I wondered if he would hate
What had become, "of his fate"

But! "believing" on the other hand,
He's no longer, of this land

But! "in heaven" "at God's right hand"
And now! Mike! can, "sweep just sand"

8-27-1997

Reflections

I wondered why!
So quiet, this guy

With time, to relax and reflect
He thought "Oh what the heck!"

With pole in hand,
He left the land

To join, "the spirits of the sea"
And have, "the fish come to thee"

Fin by fin,
They did pour in!

So many fish, of a different kind,
It liked to blow my mind!

His thoughts, they did run wide,
With feelings, he could not hide

I know this man, with the smile, on his face
He walks, with thee, in grace

Oh! "thank You Lord" for his gentle touch
You know! it means, so very much

To have you bless, my special place,
And put a smile, on every face

His days of fishing, "they were bliss"
"When it's time to go", "his presence I will miss"

"But memories", "there are to hold"
"Treasure", "them like shining gold"

"Thank You Lord" for, "blessings of rhyme"
Here in this place, "somewhere in time"

9-15-1997

Thank You
Vic & Judy Baus

Spirits Dancing

The day, two spirits met
Their, fate was set

As they, drew near
There was "nothing to fear"

For there was "a warmness" in the "heart and soul"
That "they could not control"

A warmth, that "covered their very being"
And, that not many others, were seeing

Their "spirits dancing" in "the moon light"
Oh! "what a beautiful sight"

Without, "uttering a sound"
They, "danced all around"

Not! "in each other's arms to hold"
But! "in the spirit" "bright and bold"

Their, "spirits" "dancing in the moonlight"
As if, "they would take flight"

9-17-1997

God's Office Door

His office, has an open door,
You never, have to, pace the floor

Or wait, to come inside,
For His door, and arms, are open wide

If you look around, to see Him there,
He's not, just there, He's everywhere

The heart, is where, He likes, to hide,
So! open it big, and give Him a ride

When you finally, let Him aboard,
You'll find, you're never bored

Life! you will see, with a different view,
As all things, are made anew

This life He gave,
Now He will save

We'll make that passage, by and by,
And be in heaven, way on high

So! the day, the door, is opened wide,
And! He stands saying, "come inside"

Don't make Him wait!
Don't hesitate!

For you are about, to take, a heavenly flight
To a most, glorious warm, bright, heavenly light

Wrapped! in the warmth, of an angel white
She'll! carry you, to God's Holy Light

So remember, God's, office door,
You'll not find it, on the second floor

It's already, in, the heart full, of pride,
When you, remember to open wide

God's Holy Spirit, will jump inside,
And there with, He will abide

For: James & Kimberly Riffle

5-1-1998

Full Circle

He met the beauty, of his life
This lady, he made his wife

They both, were very wise
And life was one, big surprise

With their, daughters two
Life's troubles, they were few

But life, changed, so quick
This lady of beauty, became sick

The wonder, of their life, so fair
Now lay, in need, of loving care

They watched, as she slipped, away
That, fateful day

She, floated away, like a feather
As, the family, they did gather

Her beauty, to restore
When she reaches, heaven's door

Almost twenty-four years, to the very day
Down the aisle, she came his way

To place, there, the golden, wedding bands
Now! he places, her, in God's hands

She once wrote, while still of these lands
"How safe, she felt, in God's hands"

To her, her angel, did fly
To carry her, to heaven on high

Oh! by the way, did I mention?
She now lay, in the garden of ascension

Alpha & Omega

The beginning & the end

IN MEMORY OF KIMBERLY LORRAINE (NICHOLS) RIFFLE
Dedicated to:
Husband - James A. Riffle, Daughter - Amanda N. Riffle
Daughter - Heather R. Riffle, Mother - Barbara J. Riffle
Born: 5-5-1956, Died: 9-11-1998
Married: 9-15-1974, Buried: 9-15-1998

9-12-1998

My Child of God

By a river she stands, the water so clear
With long curly hair, blowing in the breeze
She moves about, with such grace and ease

Restored to the beauty of her youth
She walks through gardens of rare flowers
Never seen by eyes on this place called Earth
She walks for hours

She dances and sings, like an angel so light
No scars, no hint of the madness, that took her life
Her joy's in God's light so bright

She greets the people, as she dances by
With a beautiful, twinkle in her eye

A scent brushes! across her nose
As she pauses to smell a rose

She picks an orchid for her hair
Never so happy, never so fair

She dances on the quilting frame
Set aside just for her in the sparkling sun
To sew the quilt she had no time to do
With magnificent colors, never done

She was promised an eternity,
An eternity it will take
All her masterpieces, to create,
She will leave in her wake

As he promised, waiting with loved ones
Who went before
Just creating her masterpiece, biding her time
Waiting for many, many more

Loved ones who miss her and can't wait to see
The beauty of her and her masterpiece to be

By: Barbara Biles
Mother of Kimberly Lorraine (Nichols) Riffle

1-9-1999

The Valley Green

Along the valley floor,
The road leads to an open door

Nestled in this valley green,
Along side a rustling stream

Was the little tower bells call to all,
As it echoed along the valley wall

Like soldiers they all line the road,
All the cars in which they rode

People's praise of God's Holy Word,
Along the valley the echoes can be heard

How peaceful our valley green,
A beauty most have not seen

2-09-2000

CHAPTER III

SPECIAL MEMORIES

A Star (By Danny Lee Husk)	77
A Daughter's Call	79
My Daughter's Thoughts	80
Raven's Feather	82
So I'll Carry These Flowers	
(By Johnny Ray Husk)	83
Sammy And The Sheriff (By Don DuMond)	84
By Day's End	87
Gator Bay	89
Kitty Dear	90
I'll Be There Tomorrow	91
New Home	93
Old Friends	95
Dear Friend	96
The Pier	97
Spirits Flow	99
Golden Memories	101
The Lady In White	103
Stan By Night	104
Friend Of A Friend	106

A Star

I saw, a star, last night
A star, that shone, so bright

It seemed, to smile, at me a bit
Through the dark, of night, around it

To myself, I silently, wonder
Was that, your star, twinkling up yonder

The beauty, of it, shining bright
It lit, your magic, and charm, by night

If to again, see your star
I'll know, you're watching, from afar

That you'll forever, and always be
In the heavens, silently, watching, over me

And when, my star, to me, is given
I want it, next, to yours, in heaven

So, the brilliant light, we then give
Can be seen, by everyone, as long as, they live

To: Gloria Jean Powers
From: Danny L. Husk Sr.

11-24-1970

I had kept the poem for years, and then in 1986, we went to the Florida Keys. While on a sunset cruise, a cloud appeared; it was unreal.

A Daughter's Call

At a daughter's call
You know, she must have had a fall

As a small child
She was quite wild

But as a teen
She was not, quite so mean

As she became a lady
Her childhood, became shady

As she became a mother
She's as good as any other

As a wife
She has dedicated her life

10-2-1995

My Daughter's Thoughts

I can afford
To thank the Lord

For the times, I've had
With! my mom and dad

They've kept me, from strife
All! of my life

Regrets! I have none
As! I watched, them become one

They have been, together
Through! all kinds, of weather

Since, the early days
Quite! "set" in their ways

To see them, so in love
It fits them, like a glove

I can't compare
The life, that they share

It means, so much
To see, their gentle touch

My respect, they do gain
To see them, bent in pain

Still! with love, in their eyes
They are, so wise

Their love, you can't miss
As they give, a gentle kiss

With that, special love, in their heart
They're seldom apart

They're two of a kind
With each other, in mind

They're hardly, ever sad
And they never, stay mad

I'm so glad
You are, my mom and dad

Your influence, on my life
Made me, a better mother and wife

I and my brothers
Think! you are, like no others

11-24-1995

Raven's Feather

I saw a raven, fly over head
With a message, I fear, I dread

A dreadful gloom
Filled the room

As there was, scorn
That, dreadful morn

As the message came in
From next of kin

Old feelings, deep inside
That we must hide

About someone, so far, from the heart
Who can always, tear us apart

Maybe one day, our hearts will mend
And no longer, have to pretend

Maybe then, we'll fly free,

As the flight of a raven's feather
And we'll, draw closer together

1-21-1996

So I'll Carry These Flowers

This is just one, of life's mysteries, you see.
Just remember, I'm where I should be.

Heartfelt moments to be.
I'll gather like flowers, to carry with me.

Now! I'll walk through life, with my flowers at hand.
Thinking how life, could be so grand.

Although a real flower, may wither away.
These I carry, to share one day.

What brought us together now sends us apart.
So with these flowers, goes my heart.

By: Johnny Ray Husk

8-21-1995

Years ago, I had given my son Johnny a copy of my book as it was then. When I got it back, this poem that he had written was in the back of it. Johnny, thank you.

Sammy and The Sheriff

    Don had asked me once if I was going to add this one of his to my collection. "I thought for a minute" "sure! Why not! If you want to!" "Well here it is, and what a story."

It was a lukewarm day
On the sixth of May,
When we rolled into the park.
An oasis for RVs
This place called "Gulf Breeze",
Tween Carrabelle and Lanark

I had reserved a nice spot
Just across from the dock,
With a beautiful view of the shore
Where the white sugar sand
And the gulf water so grand,
Would be 50 feet from the door.

But alas and alack,
I was taken aback,
By the scene which met my eye.
For my spot had been taken
My poor heart was ach-in,
And my wife was about to cry.

Then along came the sheriff
To pick up his tariff,
His little black dog on a leash.
They walked through the sand

Plastic bag in Bob's hand,
So Sammy wouldn't foul the beach.

Please sheriff I cried
As I rushed to his side,
Remove these folks from my place.
But he made no reply,
Not a flick of his eye,
Nor expression at all on his face

For his attention was set
On his little black pet,
Whose rear was aimed at the ground.
Then "Rats", a false start
And a pitiful fart,
Was all that came out of that hound

Hurry up and be done
You son of a gun,
I yelled at the poor little gnome.
While you're hesitating
My poor wife is waiting,
To move in her brand new home.

"Except no reply"
Sheriff said with a sigh,
Twill do you no good to moan.
Though it might do some good
If hear you he could,
But Sammy is deaf as a stone.

Then as if he had heard
Sammy let go a turd,
That dog was not playing fair.
But the sheriff was faster

And avoided disaster,
By snagging that bomb in midair

Then he said to me "Son
My job here is done"
Now I'll tend to that jerk.
And then when I'm through
I'll have me a brew,
Being sheriff is sure thirsty work.

Now my life is at ease
Living here at "Gulf Breeze",
So secure in my own little yard.
For I know come what may
I'll be safe night and day,
With Sammy and the sheriff on guard

By - Don DuMond

Copyright: 5-6-1994

    I, Gloria, am adding the conclusion to this story of Sammy and the sheriff. Don really got a kick out of this pair. For the time that Don and his family were at the park it was called Gulf Breeze; it is now Ho Hum RV Park. I had notified Don of the results. Poor little Sammy, the faithful companion of the sheriff Don spoke of, passed over into Doggie Heaven September 1996. As for the sheriff (Robert "Bob" Emerson), he went to be with The Lord September 9, 1997, the very next year after Sammy. I did the poem "The Gatekeeper" after he passed on; it was so fitting of him, and it was used as the eulogy at his service. Bob was cremated and his ashes were spread at sea five mile straight out off the end of the pier at the east end of Dog Island, by Danny Husk, Howard Adams, Marty Roller and Chopps Foster. A swing was erected by Mike Hughes, the owner of the RV park, in his favorite setting place with a plaque donated by friends Pete and Carwe Sherrod mounted in the top of it. Many people have enjoyed that swing over the years; for all we know "Ole Bob might be sitting right there with them."
"We Love You Bob."

By Day's End

On this spring day
They were on their way

Going along, feeling great
As they traveled, down Ninety-Eight

Hearing a "click and a clatter"
They wondered! what was the matter?

With "emotions in a mix"
There was a "starter" to fix

Now to have some fun
With work all done

So with the beach, within their reach

Now! thought things, to be grand
But now! they get stuck, in the sand

So now! without a doubt
A wrecker, pulled them out

By now, the day was getting hot
So they found another spot

Now! that things, had settled down
They threw, a blanket, on the ground

Now! in the sun, they had their fun
Until, the day was done

And there, "their eyes met"
A "most beautiful" "sunset"

4-11-1996

Gator Bay

As I was looking out
I gave a shout

I tell no lies
A pair of eyes

There came my way
From across the bay

As they came nearer
It became clearer

It was a gator
I learned later

He swam around
Without a sound

His body long and lean
And seldom seen

When he saw me
He did flee

7-10-1996

Kitty Dear

A lady, named Kitty, their twas
The sweetest person, ever was

She comes to visit, once a year
And everyone, loves her dear

I gave a stuffed kitty
To this lady, so pretty

She! like a kitten
It seemed quite fit-in'

We have a boat
On the bay afloat

On which Kitty! did ride!
Across the bay! so wide!

But there came, a day, to sigh!
The day! she had to say! "goodbye"!

8-14-1996

I'll Be There Tomorrow

There would come a day
When he would be on his way

Headed for his special place
That always brought a smile to his face

This place to him was nice
Just his little paradise

But somehow along the way
There came an "unexpected delay"

A delay! of an order he had been given
It was now! his time to come to heaven

But! with "the love of this place in his heart"
For a bit, he could not part

He called a friend, to tell of his sorrow
But instead "said" "I'll be there tomorrow"

But! "tomorrow" came and went
And off! to "heaven he had been sent"

But sadness, I do lack
For I know! his "spirit" will be back

To walk along, the white sugar sand beach
That he tried so "desperately" to reach

11-17-1996

New Home

There came to, our park one day
A couple from far away

They had looked, "far and wide"
Moving around, "like the tide"

They looked for, "a place to call home"
So they would, "never more roam"

One day they did, decide to stay
And for the park, "they did pay"

To live here by the bay
And walk the beach every day

Now this "couple" and their "kitties two"
Can enjoy the "great view"

Now! the park that was in much "strife"
Is now coming back! to "life"

With their hard work, I know they can
Fulfill their "dream and plan"

But if! "some day"
They decide, to go "their way"

A bit of them! "will stay"
To warm our, "hearts every day"

12-27-1996

Old Friends

Today I heard a voice from the past
Who told of a love that didn't last

A love that started way back when
Things were simpler then

But life is always in a state of change
And plans can only be short range

The voice I heard that day
I recognized right away

As that of a dear friend
Reaching out from the other end

I hope soon there will come a day
When I can hear him say

Come give me a big hug
A big one warm and snug

5-5-1997

Dear Friend

Are you still there?
Or are you locked inside somewhere?

There used to be a "little smile"
That I've not seen for "quite awhile"

Now upon your face
A "distant look" takes its place

Your warm and bubbly presence, is gone I feel
Now replaced, with cold gray steel

"What happened"? to that friend I knew
Now it seems, she is always blue

With me I feel, she may be "annoyed"
And "maybe" trying to "avoid"

But "maybe" "none of this is true"
And "one day", things will be "anew"

And I'll "hear a familiar phrase"
Such as "damn it!" "I hate these dreary days!"

2-16-1997

The Pier

It wasn't hard to find
The plans he had in mind

As polls went into place
The pier took on a brand new face

With the laying of the planks
I gave a very grateful thanks

Then to make it plumb
A cord was pulled, to where it started from

Along the cord the wind did blow
And from it sweet sounds did flow

The song I heard that day
Was the song of life on its way.

Now as it again comes to life
I pray it will be kept from strife

A walk down its long golden aisles
Brought a tear to my eyes, that soon turned to a smile

It put a smile on Mike's face
To put the pier back in its place

P.S. please God let it hang around and not get knocked back down.

Sadly, the following August hurricane Earl blew in and took off the whole deck end of it and part of it at the land. It wasn't long though and it was good as new, thanks to Mike Hughes, the owner of the park. Many a GREAT DAY spent fishing from that pier at Ho-Hum RV Park, Carrabelle, Florida.
http://www.hohumrvpark.com

5-26-1997

Spirits Flow

I met a guy the other day
Who was passing my way

He seemed to be carrying, a heavy load
As he traveled down, that long road

With the only thing, to keep him sane
Was his, being so humane

He never sat around, like bumps on logs
For traveling with him, were his dogs

With a little down time, at hand
They would play, in the sand

And I never knew
Who would out do who

They would swim and play
Half the day

This guy's name, I found, to be Joe
And with a bottle, of Jack Daniels in tow

With some time to kill
And a glass to fill

I couldn't sneeze
At a chance, to shoot the breeze

With Jimmy Buffett, playing loud
My heart sounds, to surely draw a crowd

With the music and the drink
There was a lot of time to think

To search for the truth
Of a lost youth

Where the feelings grow
And the spirits flow

I think of how, it might have been
Way back when

The feelings, can still be found
But those days are no longer around

Thank you Joe!
For the spirits flow

From the feelings I know
You made my spirits glow
And many tears to flow

7-14-1997

Golden Memories

Word came down the other day
That family was on the way

So many thoughts of a different kind
Began to fill his mind

Memories were held like gold
As thoughts began to unfold

After a long drive
Word came they had arrived

His heart in his throat
It was hard to speak a note

From down the beach
They all came within his reach

It was such a great treat
To hear their voices so sweet

They had come from far and near
His mother and three sisters dear

The collected memories of gold
All then started to unfold

They reminisced of the past
And of new memories to last

They have had much fun
But soon will have to run

By the time they had to go
My emotions I tried not to show

But the tears they did start
From all that I felt in my heart

In-laws sometimes can be a pain
But with mine I would like to remain

The times were good for those few days
And will be missed in many ways

But a picture of them I find
Locked in the back of my mind

    A surprise visit to my husband Danny from three of his sisters and his mother, who came down from Parkersburg, West Virginia and stayed at the hotel down the way and walked up the beach to meet us as we walked down from Ho Hum RV Park where we lived at the time.
    It was a GREAT REUNION for all!

8-10-1997

The Lady in White

By the pale moon light
Stands the lady in white

A ghostly shadow moves through the house
Being quiet as a mouse

I know I have nothing to fear
For she used to live here

There lingers across the nose
The scent of a beautiful rose

Was this lady of such refine
Still living in another time

What I she could be set free
Should that be up to me

12-19-1998

Stan by Night

The mystery man, known, as "Stan"

Who was this stranger?
We all thought, to be in danger

With computers, he did work
Oh! how, he cut up, like a crazy jerk

In our mind, there was no doubt
Of this man, we had come to care about

This man, was thought, to be quite fair
So he was asked, to run for mayor

When the day came, to take a vote
Things ended, on a sour note

Discouraged, not, this man of ours
For he, had a new plan, within hours

One day, we did frown
For a new job, took him out of town

Every, now and then, to our delight
He'll drop by, to spend the night

Now he's known, as "Stan by night"
Ready, to pick up, and take flight

But! never fear,
For he will! reappear

In our, extra bed
A place, to rest, his "weary head"

"Good night Stan" "our computer man"

8-19-2000

Friend of A Friend

As your friend's wife,
You came into my life,

You seemed like, such a mystery,
Not knowing, your history

A guy! looking back, with no remorse,
A guy! who always, seeming to be on course

A new business, you did start,
Of which, we sort of, became a part

Although I didn't let it show,
Closer to you my feelings grow

Then you say you're going to leave,
And my heart starts to grieve

Oh! how it makes me feel, so low,
To think I won't hear you say, "hello"

In a very special way,
I love and miss you every day

A good friend to me,
You'll be, as I pray; I'll be to thee

12-15-1999

CHAPTER IV

LOVE IS FREE

Morning Glory	109
Of Love and Death (By Don DuMond)	111
Moon Lovers	113
A Moment in Time	114
Good-Bye My Love	117
Missing You	119
Your Touch	120
Our Days	121
Without You	123
A Flight of Love	125
Dove Of Love	127
What If	128
Dream Traveler	130
My Blue Heaven	131
The Scent of You	132
Take Time to Smell the Roses	133
Lost But Not Forgotten	135

Morning Glory

When I woke, you were, on my mind
And I had to remember, how sweet and kind

Time has taken us apart
But you, are always in my heart

Today while, I was reading a book
And hearing, "the angels among us" I had a message, they took

The words aren't, hard to find
Cause I can't, get them out, of my mind

Today I heard, the words of a poet
No truer words, were ever spoke, I know it

It is hard to find
A love so sweet and kind

There would be days, that I wonder, was it fate?
Or has the universe? Given me a soul mate

I know that it doesn't matter
But I prefer, the latter

As the sun set
I'm so glad, that we met

As the moon crosses the bay
I thank, the universe for another day

11-18-1994

Of Love and Death

I read today that Johnny died,
He had only nineteen years.
Although I didn't know the lad,
I had to shed some tears.

For I have just turned thirty-eight,
And those tears I wept for me.
But twas not for sorrow that I cried,
They were tears of joy you see.

Although our end is all the same,
And we have one life to be;
I'm glad twas Johnny on that plane,
And my journey is by the sea.

Not that I'm afraid to die,
Or that I even mind;
But if my years were cut in half,
Your love I'd never find.

Of course I never would have known
The joy that I'd be missing.
And the comfort of your tender arms
Or the lips that I've been kissing.

But now that I have found you,
The one that I love so,

I want to live eternally;
I never want to go.

But alas, the trip must end;
The port could be quite near.
So I will just enjoy our love,
While both of us are here.

Then, if I die tomorrow,
I ask you shed no tears.
For unlike that boy Johnny,
I had you plus nineteen years.

By: Don DuMond

Copyright: 1995

Moon Lovers

The moon is as bright, as a shining star
To show the world, how fair you are

But you light up the night
Like the brightest light

As we walk hand in hand down the lane
You my darling, keep me sane

For you brought me out of the dark
Now life with you, is like a walk in the park

12-19-1994

A Moment in Time

There was a place in time
That was not mine

An empty place
That had no face

Then one day, the forces that be
Brought you to me

Your life, within me, dwells
But to no one, I could not tell

For fear, if I would
I would be, misunderstood

So within me, it slept
While at times, I wept

And again, I had to say good-bye
And deep inside, I felt I would die

A cold day, in November
I can't help, but to remember

A good friend, took his final sleep
And all I could do is weep

During that time of pain and grief
From deep inside, I screamed, for you, for relief

And like magic, one day
I was on my way

And as we were reunited
I knew, I could not fight it

The powers that be
Had sent you to me

And there was a moment, I swear!
That I was totally aware

That even in a crowd
Our voices spoke loud

As everyone gazed
They were amazed

That as our spirits flowed
And at how we glowed

And at that moment, there was no fright
When we both, became one light

Of this feeling, I thought would be never
But now I know, our souls are forever

No greater feeling, there can be told
Than this one, that I hold

This empty place
Now has a face

With so much love
Sent from above

As the feelings we have are fine
As we meet "somewhere in time"
I am yours and you are mine

1-8-1995

Good-Bye My Love

He came to me, in the still of night
And gave me, no fright

Standing, in the bright rays, of the moon
So bright, it might, have been noon

He stood there, looking so divine
He reached out, his hand, to mine

He took, my hand, in his with grace
And such, soft embrace

We soared, like an eagle, in flight
Up to the greatest height

Pulling me, close to, his chest
I felt the beat, of his heart, in his breast

Like the strum,
Of a bass drum

He ran, his fingers, through my hair
So long, so gold, and fair

Whispering, to each other
You are, my lover,

I stood, in tears
As, I realized, my greatest fears

A love, that wasn't, meant to be
Is all, it can be, to me

So, instead of, saying hi!
All! we can do, is say "good-bye"
"I'll always love you" "Good-bye"

1-24-1995

Missing You

As I look out, across the bay
I miss you more, every day

As I see, the birds fly
I remember our, last good-bye

As the waters, flow
I see your, warm glow

To see the sun, shine so bright
I wish again, to hold you tight

To see a, new hatch
I know, will bring, fish to catch

But the sea, is a lonely place
Without your, friendly face

Today I yearn
For your return

A day of "great joy"
Will be, to hear you call, "Ahoy"

2-14-1995

Your Touch

When winter days, are long, and cold
The thought of you, is what, I hold

I long, to hold you, very much
You know! I miss your gentle touch

Enclosed in your, big strong arms
I feel protected, from all harms

The touch, of your sweet embrace
From my mind, I can not erase

You touched my heart, you touched my mind
No better friend, I could not find

2-18-1995

Our Days

Our days, at the shore,
Have made me soar

It makes me feel, young and gay
To run along the beach, and play

As we stroll, hand in hand
The sounds around, play like a band

The gentle roll, of the tide
As we look across, the bay so wide

The little slap,
Of a white cap

Whether early or late,
The call of a gull, to his mate

To see a mullet,
Try to jump! from a pelican's gullet

As we float,
Along in the boat

You can see on the horizon,
The sun is rising

As we go along and dream,
Of that island, in the stream

I am so glad, we have had, our day,
To have the time, to play

Cause I know, there will be
A day to look back and see, what it meant to me

And as the sun sets,
None of our days do I regret

So till the day we part
I will hold, "our days" dear in my heart

2-28-1995

Without You

There are days, of gray and blue
When all I do, is think of you

The days, are so long
Since you been gone

Even though, you're far away
You're in my heart, every day

Our love is like a flower
That blooms, with every, waking hour

As I sit and yearn, for your return

To feel, your warm touch
Will pleasure, me much

It will be, so nice
To have you back, in our paradise

To others, it may not be, the same thing
But to me, life it brings

I thank, the powers, that be
For sending, you to me

But I know there will! come a day
When, they take you away

And it will be, sad but true
To have to spend, my days, without you

In so many ways
I will love you always

3-16-1995

A Flight of Love

As I lie, looking at the stars, last night
They lit! the sky, with all their might

As I watched, I thought of you, my love
You came swooping, like a dove

You picked! and carried me up, me away
Until we saw, the break of day

We soared! so high
The stars, were like diamonds, in the sky

As we soared! through, time and space
I saw, the love, in your face

Soaring! up so high! I saw the clouds, go rolling by
Somehow, I knew, our love, would never die

As you hold me, close to your heart
I know, we'll never part

I know, you were sent, from up above
To seal, our undying love

I felt, so much bliss
At the touch, of your tender kiss

At day's, break
I, awake

To find, you've flown! into the night
Where another time, we'll join in flight
But until then, I'll love you, with all my might

3-22-1995

Dove of Love

You came to me, in the dead of night
I gave up, without a fight

With hearts, on fire
Of your love, I will never tire

As our love, flows!
Your closeness, forever grows

Your love, is so gentle, and kind
It's not just, a state of mind

Our love
Is like, the sweet, sound of a dove

With every, coo
I think, of you

We'll never, be apart
You're forever, in my heart

5-3-1995

What If

What if the sun, didn't shine
Would you? still, be mine

What if I were, blue
I would, think of you

What if I were, sad
Would you make me glad

What if I were, sick
Would you stick

What if I said, I love you
Would it? be true

What if I told you, it makes no diff.
Because, I don't believe, in what if

I believe, in love
And the heavens above

A big hug
To feel warm and snug

The gentle, touch
That means, so much

I love you more, every day
So much, that you, take my breath away

5-8-1995

Dream Traveler

Across, the country, I travel
On roads, both paved, and gravel

Over, the next hill
Is a part, of life, to fill

But travel, as I might
I long, to hold, you tight

The days, are long, and lonely
Thinking! of you only

Soon! my travel, will be done
And then, "we'll," be as one

So! keep dreaming, of the day
We meet again, down life's highway

7-7-199

My Blue Heaven

I've been given
A piece of heaven

My place in the mountain
To be there, the days, I'm count-in

My mind, oh! how it does wonder
To be back, in the hills, up yonder

And at the break of day, when I awake
I look across, the clear blue lake

But! with the new morn
My! thoughts of you are torn!

I can not! hide!
My want, for you, by my side

But! I will find, peace of mind
In the thoughts, and ties that bind

Our thoughts and spirits, they reach out
Across the mountains, there's no doubt

So till the day, I hold you near
My thoughts, I do hold dear

5-2-1996

The Scent of You

As the fog rolled in, over the bay
On that beautiful day

And the call of the loon
It ended, way to soon

There! came upon the air
A presence, so warm and fair

Just ahead, down the beach
But! always just out of reach

There was "the smell of flowers"
That! "haunted my soul" for hours

Were you there? "my love"
"Haunting me" like "the coo of a dove"

Your voice, "still lingers in my ear"
I know! "in my heart you're ever near"

1-4-1997

Take Time to Smell the Roses

As kids, we would be
Foot loose and fancy free

School days, they were a blast
But! They weren't meant to last

Friends, they came along so fast
But none of them, did last

Like sisters, we would stay
Side by side, all the way

Through, all the strife
Through, out our life

So when I was told
My heart turned cold

To my question, came an answer
I was told, that she had cancer

My niece, my friend
Us two! till the bitter end

Words! don't come easy, for me to say
But! it will, get better, along the way

"Kim" "touched our heart and soul"
And filled, within us, an empty hole

Like the pied piper, with his fife
She made you believe, in her bravery, pride and love of life

Her light! would always, shine so bright
As a beacon, in the night

To see God's Love
Shine! through her, from above

And reach out, to touch the ones she loved
And wrap around, them like a glove

With her failing health, she could hardly speak
To show her feelings, a little tear she would leak

With that one little tear, more precious than gold
My heart turned warm, now no longer cold

Sitting by her, for days on end
Knowing! she had a message to send

A message without words that rang through
A message! of hope and I love you

"Kim's love" has touched us all
She'll be there, even if we fall

And now! on the other side, she will wait
Till! we pass through, that pearly gate

1-10-1999

Lost But Not Forgotten

I have to, tell you a story
Filled, with hope and glory

About, a young lady, who didn't dawdle
For you see, she is a model

From early on
She works, from dusk to dawn

Her mom and dad,
Know, it's no fad

So with, no tears,
They, gave her, two years

She's worked hard,
Both here and abroad

Then one day, after a shoot
They gathered, their loot

While, driving along, that day
They were hit, with dismay

The thought! went up, like a red flag
Oh! my gosh! we forgot a bag

So with no, time to waste,
Away! they did haste

Now, things are grand,
With bag, in hand

Now, they make their way
Down, life's great highway

Thanks! she says, to her mother
You are, like no other

And I will, sure be glad
To see, dear ol' Dad

Who, while they were gone
Was working, on the lawn

With bushes, to trim
The light, is growing dim

A fire, burns bright
As it, lights up the night

While standing, around the fire
Dreaming, of his heart's, desire

With, words of love
His voice, reached out, from above

Which, I found
Had, a loving, sound

A sound, I felt, so deep
That, it made me weep

My feelings, I had to reach
So I took a walk, on the beach

And by now I hope, the girls are home
Never, more to roam

With, bags in tow
And nowhere else, to go

Love you all,
Both short and tall

4-15-1995

CHAPTER V

TOGETHER ONCE AGAIN

A Very SPECIAL DEDICATION to my Sister	141
A Special Prayer	142
A Whisper	143
God's Own Time	144
God's Special Touch	145
Great Expectations	146
The Ties That Bind	147
Troubled Times	148

A Very SPECIAL DEDICATION To My Sister

"One Half of the 'Two Peas in a Pod'—Gloria Here"
I live in Lanark Village on the Gulf of Mexico, in the Florida Panhandle (http://www.apalachicola.com/).

This poem came to be with a renewed relationship with my half sister, Pamela Mae (Powers) Moore, after thirty-five years being separated. We had first made contact through e-mail and then she and her husband, Verlin Lee (Mike) Moore, came to Florida for a visit and get to know each other.

Come to find out we were so much alike it was unreal; our husbands said we were just like "two peas in a pod."

I also have two "great" half brothers and two more "beautiful" half sisters that Pam has helped me to get back in touch with.

"Thank God for small favors"
I LOVE YOU ALL.

A Special Prayer

"GOD THANK YOU" for this day
Protect my sister on her way

Please guide our heart
As a, new friendship, got its start

Let our will, be yours

And heal the hurt of time

"THANK YOU LORD" for letting this be
A very special time for me

So many years, we had to wait
"OH! and thanks" for not taking me through,"that pearly gate"

I know You had, something else in mind
In the future for us to find

"THANK YOU LORD" for keeping us in mind
And for a sister, so sweet, so gentle and kind

Our lives will never be the same
As we "PRAISE YOUR HOLY NAME"

"THANK YOU JESUS"

5-20-1999

A Whisper

Can a "whisper", mean so much?
As much, as "a gentle touch"

To hear a "soft sweet voice"
Above all the noise

A soft sweet sound
"That wraps you, all around"

Like being wrapped, "in an angel's arms"
Protecting you, from all harms

"The sweetest sound", I ever knew
Three simple words, "I LOVE YOU"

5-26-1999

God's Own Time

Why did we have to wait so long?
For such a life, to come along

It was always such a strain
To hold the heart ache and the pain

The thought of my siblings in such pain
I cast from my mind and start again

But every now and then, it would reappear
Bringing back all, the doubt and fear

But God has a reason, for everything
Now let's see! what He will bring

God! We know, that times were hard
Thank You! For always standing guard

Thank You for a family so dear
Even if we could never be near

But! even so far apart
"THEY'RE ALWAYS IN MY HEART"

5-25-1999

God's Special Touch

Can two people so far apart?
Be held together, with each other's heart

Can the love and concern, within their mind
Be what holds, the ties that bind

Like twins, separated at birth
They go through life, upon this earth

With the feeling of an empty place
That transcends, all time and space

But one day! "they" will understand
"When God opens" "His Mighty Hand"

Then all the knowledge will come pouring out
Then of their life, there will no doubt

For in, "God's own masterful way"
"He opens! Their eyes one day"

5-26-1999

Great Expectations

Now these two people, so full of woe!
Now have a new direction, in which to go

Their pain, they hope, will be no more
As now! their spirits, they can soar

For now their lives are so entwined
It almost, "boggles the mind"

Their new life, they live, from day to day
And "cherish it" "in a special way"

"The feelings" that they share
Not many people, can compare

All the emotions of the years
Have been released in tears

Now there is, some doubt and fear
As that awaited, day draws near

4-29-1999

The Ties That Bind

What are? the ties that bind!
Is it all, just in our mind?

There is a place, in my mind, I can recall
Where all bad memories, tend to fall

But somewhere, in that space of gray
Bad things, will be set free, I pray!

A lifetime "haunted" by the past
Can now be, set free at last

No more wonder, fear and doubt
All bad things, are now cast out!

We never know, which way, our lives will turn
But in our hearts, for the truth we yearn!

If you want the truth, to set you free
Then just leave it, "up to thee"

Long ago! It was written, "in the book"
The right time, place and "GOD IS ALL IT TOOK"

4-5-1999

Troubled Times

We went through life, in our own separate way
Two lives! that would come together, one day!

Two people, so far away from each other
Neither having the same mother

But! that's not all bad!
For you see they had the same dad!

Separated as children, so long ago
Full of desperation and woe!

This heart was torn, from this little life!
Being afraid for her and all the strife!

As years went by, I would wonder why?

Why life had been so hard
And never allowed, to drop our guard

3-25-1999

To end...

They may have been troubled times back then in the beautiful hills of West Virginia, but the greatest thing of all, we grew up in God's Love and going to church most every Sunday, also grew up in one of the BIGGEST and GREATEST FAMILIES that God ever put on this earth.

My very best memories are growing up in this family until the age of sixteen when I left home.

All my love to my whole family for the year I had with them. I love you! Momma "Oneita" and Daddy "Glenn Powers." Sincerely this has been a great journey.

Gloria Jean Powers